FIND YOUR POWER

TAROT

An Hachette UK Company
www.hachette.co.uk

First published in Great Britain in 2023 by Godsfield,
an imprint of Octopus Publishing Group Ltd
Carmelite House, 50 Victoria Embankment, London EC4Y 0DZ
www.octopusbooks.co.uk

ISBN 978-1-8418-1536-7

A CIP catalogue record for this book is available from the British Library

Printed and bound in China

10 9 8 7 6 5 4 3 2 1

Publisher: Lucy Pessell
Designer: Isobel Platt
Senior Editor: Hannah Coughlin
Assistant Editor: Samina Rahman
Production Controller: Allison Gonsalves
Illustrations: p. 13, 21, 120 created by Imogen Oh from the Noun Project

The 78 plates illustrating the Major and Minor Arcana are from designs by Pamela Colman Smith, reproduced from
the unabridged Dover 2005 republication of the edition published by William Rider & Son Limited, London, 1911 under
the title *The Pictorial Key to the Tart: Being Fragments of a Secret Tradition under the Veil of Divination*

FIND YOUR POWER

TAROT

ERIN REGULSKI

GODSFIELD

CONTENTS

INTRODUCING THE TAROT	8
HOW TO USE YOUR CARDS	14
THE MAJOR ARCANA	28
THE MINOR ARCANA	52
CARD SPREADS AND STORIES	112
GOING DEEPER	122

FIND YOUR POWER

When daily life becomes busy and your time and energy is pulled in many different directions, it can be difficult to find time to nourish yourself. Prioritizing your own wellbeing can be a struggle and you risk feeling overwhelmed, unsure of where to turn and what you need in order to feel lighter and find your inner strength.

Taking some time to focus on yourself, answering questions you may be avoiding or facing problems that are simmering away under the surface is the best gift you can give yourself. But it can be difficult to know where to start.

Sometimes all you need to learn life's big lessons is a little guidance. In this series of books you will learn about personal healing, self empowerment and how to nourish your spirit. Explore practices which will help you to get clear on what you really want, and that will encourage you to acknowledge – and deal with – any limiting beliefs or negative thoughts that might be holding you back to living life to your fullest power.

These pocket-sized books provide invaluable advice on how to create the best conditions for a healthier, happier, and more fulfilled life Bursting with essential background, revealing insights and useful activities and exercises to enable yourself to understand and expand your personal practices every day, it's time to delve into your spiritual journey and truly Find Your Power.

Other titles in the series:

- *Find Your Power: Manifest*
- *Find Your Power: Numerology*
- *Find Your Power: Runes*

INTRODUCING THE TAROT

KNIGHT OF CUPS

XVIII

XVIII

THE MOON

QUEEN OF WANDS

If your life feels overwhelming, confusing or stuck, picking up a deck of Tarot cards is one of the most rewarding and creative ways to find answers. Despite its esoteric and sometimes unnerving reputation, Tarot is a friendly and enjoyable way to explore your life's journey, whoever you are and whatever you're dealing with. All you need are curiosity and a willingness to tell the truth.

What if I told you that our lives are made up of a set number of stories or patterns? Each of these stories waxes and wanes throughout our lives, becoming more dominant and less so day-by-day as our attention, moods and concerns shift and change, but we all have these stories and patterns in common: they are what unite us and make us human.

The Tarot, at its simplest, depicts 78 of these stories. Each story card holds a secret lesson or teaching,

and deciphering each card's secret is what reading the Tarot is all about. Whether these lessons apply to our present, past or future is up to us, but as we are only ever really *here*, in this moment of time, the Tarot is most useful at helping us see more clearly where we are right now. Rather than "predicting" the future, by showing us our behaviours, thoughts and blind spots, the Tarot can also help us to see where we might be headed if we don't make a change.

Think of the deck as a wise, no-nonsense friend or therapist, the kind who always seems to know the raw truth behind things, who helps you to see how you could move forward with hope and love rather than shame. You can turn to them every day no matter how you're feeling; they will never judge you and always accept you exactly as you are. I think we're all in need of a friend like that.

THE HISTORY
OF THE TAROT

Tarot cards are said to trace their meanings and origins back to the late 14th century, but are thought to have their roots in both ancient Egyptian and Greek mysticism. As long as there have been human beings, the wisest ones among us have attempted to depict and code the mysteries and truths of life. Tarot is one of the ways in which this wisdom and life experience have been passed down, with each generation's readers and teachers adding their own new perspectives.

Originally, cards were used that look much like our common playing cards. Divided into four suits – wands, cups, coins and swords – each card had a particular shared meaning associated with it, like a collection of folk tales passed from person to person. As time went by, it became the fashion to commission additional "trump" cards to add to your deck. Drawn by skilled artists, they depicted more universal themes and featured elaborate pictures of archetypal images such

as The Fool, Justice, Death, Lovers, a Hanged Man. These more famous cards are likely the ones that you are most familiar with.

It is this evolution that gave Tarot its **two main components**: the older **Minor Arcana** with its suits, numbers and court cards, and the newer 22 **Major Arcana** or trump cards. "Arcana" means mysteries or secrets. We'll learn more about the difference between these two parts of the deck on pages 28 and 52.

The Tarot deck that you've probably seen most often, and the one on which this book's readings are founded, is the Rider-Waite deck drawn by Pamela Colman Smith. First published in 1909, Smith was the first artist, as far as we know, to introduce iconic characters and scenes into the Minor Arcana cards, rather than just drawing the trumps, and her colourful and lively deck has become the template on which most modern Tarot decks are based. A resurgence of interest in Tarot in recent times has led to a growing abundance of beautiful and diverse decks for us to own and explore, but Smith's symbolism still runs deep.

Although life has changed considerably over the centuries, the fact that our brains and bodies still work in the same way means that we share a surprising amount in common with people of the past. It is in this way that the Tarot could be said to represent something universal about humanity: the dramas, pain, fears and joys that seem hardwired into us as human beings. It is these archetypes of human experience that make the Tarot as relevant and insightful today as it ever was.

GETTING STARTED

Are you ready to get to know all 78 of these wonderful stories and learn some of their secrets?

You will need:

- A full deck of Tarot cards, preferably the original Rider-Waite deck or one based on its symbolism.

- A notebook and pen.

- Some quiet time, preferably alone when you can think without distraction.

- A curious attitude. Try to drop all judgements and expectations just for a while.

I also recommend that you take some time to read this book all the way through so that you can familiarize yourself with its layout and the Tarot structure, get a sense of what to expect, and see where you might find answers to some of your questions.

HOW TO USE
YOUR CARDS

TWO OF SWORDS

THE WORLD

ACE OF CUPS

EXPLORING THE CARDS AND OURSELVES

Whether or not you've ever looked at Tarot cards before, I encourage you to take your deck and spread out all the cards in front of you. Forget the images you may have in your head of a mysterious, veiled woman laying out cards in a row for an anxious-looking querent. Forget any sense of "doing a reading" and just look. What do you see?

Do the images on the card make you smile, make your heart beat faster, feel frightening, confusing or daft? There are no wrong answers, but it can be useful to see where you're starting from.

Forget any sense of "doing a reading" and just look. What do you see?

ANXIETY

If you feel a sense of threat or worry, chances are that anxiety is going to be a companion in your readings. If you're afraid of change, feel overwhelmed by life or feel like bad news is lurking around every corner, the cards can help you with that. You can bring your anxiety to your readings and know you are safe. There are no nasty surprises waiting here, just a gentle sort of unknotting to help you look at your fears more closely. Perhaps a religious upbringing has taught you that Tarot cards are "bad". You can bring that to the cards, too. Tarot can help you look at your influences and inherited stories. See this as your chance to find out for yourself what is actually true for you.

You can bring your anxiety to your readings and know you are safe.

DOUBT

If you feel a sense of disconnection or cynicism, chances are that doubt is going to be your companion. That's OK, too – it's good to not believe everything at face value! The Tarot will allow you to be discerning and analytical and test its theories. If you're put off by the pictures, remember that they are just symbols. See them as something neutral that you can interpret however you want. Deep down, you know that you don't have all the answers. Can you accept that you might have something new to learn here?

Whatever you feel, write it out like this:

"I feel [name your feeling]. This means that [name a state of mind] is going to be with me as I read the cards."

COGNITIVE BIAS

This simple first exercise is a quick and helpful way to see what expectations, wounds and hang-ups you bring with you to your card readings. It will affect what conclusions you jump to, what you filter out and what you focus on. It is your own personal cognitive bias and is likely to make you more reactive or defensive to things that touch on it. You don't need to change how you feel or be ashamed of it – we all have biases – but if you can spot this from the start, it will be easier to see when something is getting in the way of your readings, obscuring a wider view or new perspective.

Because our biases often shift and change depending on the concerns of the day, I recommend checking in with your biases regularly.

A CARD A DAY

The best way to get to know the cards and incorporate Tarot into your life is to pick one card to focus on each day. The ideal time to do this is in the morning so you can reflect on the card as the day unfolds.

A daily practice:

1. Give your deck a good shuffle so that both the Major and Minor Arcana cards are all mixed up together.

2. Close your eyes and take a few slow breaths until you feel still and calm.

3. Ask a question, in your head or out loud. I suggest: "What do I need to see more clearly today?"

4. Spread out the cards with their backs to you, in your hands or on a table.

5. With your eyes closed, begin to touch the cards until your fingers settle on one. Pull it out and look at it.

6. Jot down your immediate reactions and associations. What thoughts and mental pictures does this card spark? How do you feel? Write this down before looking up the meaning of the card.

7. Turn to the card's listing to deepen your exploration.

8. Use the questions below to gather together your final thoughts:

> *My card today is............*
>
> *It feels relevant because............*
>
> *I feel confused about............*
>
> *I might be biased toward focusing on............*
>
> *Perhaps I also need to think about............*
>
> *My gut instinct tells me it could also mean............*
>
> *In response today, I would like to............*

ABOUT
THE CARD
INTERPRETATIONS

An interpretation of each of the Major and Minor Arcana cards is listed in the following chapters to guide your practice, but think of them as prompts rather than rules. As you read my words, what new trains of thought start to run through your mind? Look at the card again. Know that there is a story about your unique life hidden inside it. My learning and understanding come from seeing through the lens of my own life, but your life will be different. What personal wisdom and experience can you bring to the table?

CARDS REPRESENTING OTHER PEOPLE

You will notice that I have deliberately kept each card interpretation focused on *you*. This is because you are the only person whose life and choices you have full control over. It is always wisest to prioritize insight into your own nature rather than trying to second-guess other people (who you can't change anyway). That being said, our lives are interwoven with others and Tarot can act as a useful window to help you see people's patterns and behaviours from a new perspective. When you draw a card, it's worth thinking about who else the figure or figures depicted might represent. Still, remember to look with eyes of empathy rather than judgement. We all hold aspects of all of the cards. Let other people act as a mirror for your own self-learning.

FEELING
UNSAFE

Do some of the cards scare you? It's important to stress that there are no bad cards in Tarot. As you get to know them, you'll start to learn that even startling cards like Death or The Tower aren't as frightening or foreboding as you might think. If you get a sudden clench of fear, take a deep breath and remind yourself that nothing has gone wrong. However, if you find any cards to be so triggering as to cause you distress or severe anxiety, just take those cards out of the deck for a while and work with the others until you feel ready to add the triggering cards back.

FEELING
CONFUSED

It's normal to feel confused when you first look at your card, so if you feel unsure or don't get a dramatic flash of inspiration, please know that you haven't failed. Each of these stories and patterns plays themselves out in our lives all the time, whether obviously or subtly, so there can be no "wrong" card.

Sometimes the card you pick will feel uncannily relevant straight away, touching on something right at the surface of your current situation. Other cards might make you think "huh?" but don't be put off by that. All it indicates is that there is a quieter influence to learn from that you may not be conscious of. Tarot can help pull things to the foreground to make them easier to see. Think of each card acting like the focus ring on a camera, bringing one particular story into clearer view.

Often, the relevance and meaning of the cards only become clear as things start to happen and the day shifts and turns. It is common to have your "aha!" moment later in the day. On days when I've felt most confused and stuck, it has often come right before sleep when I've finally stopped and am reflecting back.

If you get a similar "aha!" moment, you might like to add your insight to your notebook (see page 13). And if you don't, just try again tomorrow with a different card. No big deal! This particular card will wait to speak to you another time.

✳

Let other people act as a mirror for your own self-learning.

✳

IS THERE
A HIGHER
POWER BEHIND
THE CARDS?

The great thing about Tarot is that you get to choose. Think of Tarot as a kind of telephone, facilitating conversation. Who would you like to talk to and receive wisdom from? Maybe you'd like to talk to your unconscious mind, or your wisest or best self. Maybe you'd like to connect with the idea of a Great Creator, nature or Mother Earth. You could talk to an ancestor or a role model or guide. If you follow a particular religion or spirituality, you can talk to your deity. If none of those appeal, you can simply treat it as a fun game of chance and explore what synchronicity arises.

To me, Tarot feels like talking to an old, wise elder with a wicked sense of humour. My cards have a tendency to be a little cheeky and no-nonsense, but always speak with warmth and love.

Don't be afraid to think about who you might be communing with. Just remember: you get to decide.

TAROT FOR GUIDANCE AND CLARITY

In our daily practice, I have suggested, "What do I need to see more clearly today?" as a question to ask, but of course you can ask any question of the cards. Here are some other questions to try:

- What insight could help me with [state your situation]?
- I'm feeling [state your feeling]. What extra information do I need to help me make a good choice today?
- I'm obsessing about [state your thoughts]. What would help me see the bigger picture?

Spend some time making a list of questions you could ask.

> **Tarot feels like talking to an old, wise elder with a wicked sense of humour.**

TAROT FOR CREATIVITY

One of the most valuable ways I've found to use Tarot in my own life is as a prompt for creativity. I'm a writer and artist and on the days when I feel stuck or blocked, the Tarot never fails to get my mind running again. So bring your work-in-progress to the cards! You could also use your daily card as a prompt for journal writing, letting it stir memories and associations. Here are some questions to ask the cards to inspire you:

- What idea or theme could I explore in my work today?

- What does my character need to learn?

- What do I need to focus on to help me get unstuck?

- What is my work missing?

REVERSE MEANINGS

You may have seen reference to "reversed" cards. This is when you draw and place a Tarot card down on a surface in front of you and see that you've placed it upside down. With a well-shuffled deck, this happens all the time. Some Tarot books even come with a whole secondary encyclopaedia of reverse meanings. Do you need to try and learn them, too?

The answer is, simply, that it's up to you. You can think of reversed cards as a kind of expansion pack for your Tarot practice: entirely optional, but interesting if you want to continue to explore Tarot in new ways.

A reversed card in your draw could mean:

- The polar opposite of the normal interpretation: literally the picture or story turned on its head. What might the opposite meaning be?

- An unexpected element, one that will make you feel especially uprooted.

- This is a card that you're particularly resistant to. What do you need to do to turn the card the right way up in your life?

- Something isn't quite what it seems and requires deeper reflection.

If you'd like to work with reversals, I have provided a question prompt for each card to get you started, but I encourage you to use your own intuition too. What darker or more obscured truth might be trying to get your attention?

THE MAJOR ARCANA

These bold cards depict life's biggest, most transformative lessons. Spread out the Major Arcana cards in order and read their descriptions and you may perceive a linear sequence or story line running through them. The Major Arcana depicts an archetypal quest, much like the one described by American writer Joseph Campbell in *The Hero with a Thousand Faces* – an analysis of the various stages of the classic hero's journey – with The Fool acting as the fresh-faced protagonist heading out the door to learn something new.

Imagine The Fool meeting each lesson in turn, being changed by it, growing and maturing a little with each card. We are The Fool, of course, and our life's path will lead us through iterations of this journey many times. Sometimes these first 22 cards are described as a circle: the revelations of The World lead us right back to start as The Fool again, new, wiser, changed. I like to think of this cycle as a spiral, each turn leading me deeper and deeper.

These bold cards depict life's biggest, most transformative lessons.

When you draw a Major Arcana card in your reading, it's time to think about where in this cycle of growth you might find yourself right now. Perhaps your card is the lesson you most need to work with and integrate next to help you find the freedom to move forward with your life.

THE FOOL

ARCANUM ZERO

Begin again

In order for our lives to change and grow, we must embrace being a beginner again. This means taking a risk that you'll look stupid, fail or get it wrong, but this is how we shake things up. It means accepting that you can't get from *here* to *there* in one leap. There will need to be many patient steps, highs and lows. The rest of the Tarot teaches how to manage the journey ahead of you. The Fool is your first nudge out the door; the call to a new adventure. Embrace the chance to start fresh.

KEYWORDS

beginnings, risk,
childlike optimism,
spontaneity, faith, boldness,
adventure, possibility

Reversed Card Question:
*'What does staying stuck
help me to avoid?'*

THE MAGICIAN

ARCANUM ONE

Use what you have

Another word for The Magician is "alchemist". This is deep creativity, turning the raw stuff of life into something new. The Magician holds all the tools of the Tarot – thoughts, feelings, energy and hard work – and knows that together they can make powerful things happen. Today, don't wait for life to give you what you want. Create it yourself. Look at what's available to you. True creativity is about working inventively with what you have, yourself included. Anything is possible with enough patience, focus and experimentation.

KEYWORDS

action, pragmatism, resourcefulness, creativity, power, self-sufficiency, manifestation, focus, alchemy, problem-solving

Reversed Card Question:
'I might be saying the right things and putting on a good show, but am I taking any real action?'

THE HIGH PRIESTESS

ARCANUM TWO

Make space and listen

What would it mean to really listen? We can be so busy talking, using our words and bodies to make sure we don't disappear, that we can fill up life with our own noise. When we choose to be quiet, we make space. Here's a chance to hear new and different voices: the quieter voice of your intuition, the wisdom of teachers, the mysterious messages of nature. What happens when you accept that you don't know all the answers, when you don't rush to fill all spaces? Be still. Listen to what speaks up when you stop.

THE HIGH PRIESTESS

KEYWORDS

wisdom, intuition, authenticity, solitude, silence, mystery, meditation, stillness, patience, guidance

Reversed Card Question:
'What am I refusing to do that I know, deep down, is right?'

THE EMPRESS

ARCANUM THREE

Be in your body

We're encouraged to live in our heads, always thinking, planning, assessing. What's below our neck is either an afterthought or something to be resented and tightly controlled. When we pay attention to our body, allowing it freedom to move and feel just as it is, we gain access to a vital creative power. Today, feel your feet on the ground. Spend time outside. Connect with your sensuality, the instincts that come from your skin and your gut. Think about what it means to be wild. How might it change you to live this way? To completely inhabit your body, however imperfect it is.

KEYWORDS

nature, self-love, self-care, sensuality, creativity, self-expression, connection, compassion, pleasure, freedom

Reversed Card Question:
'If I knew I wouldn't be judged for it, I would love to...'

THE EMPEROR

ARCANUM FOUR

Take charge

Authority is rarely comfortable. Sometimes we must step up, take control of our own lives and make decisions that affect others. These moments don't come when things feel easy. They happen when the stakes are high. Often we don't feel ready. Still, we must sit up tall in this hard, uncomfortable place and speak with strength and cool, calm conviction. Yes, you might feel scared. Yes, it might cause conflict. Authority is about having the wisdom and courage to know that you need to act anyway. You can hold all these feelings and still do the right thing.

KEYWORDS

power, control, responsibility, self-worth, leadership, truth, courage, empowerment, assertion, action

Reversed Card Question:
'What helps to shake me out of victim-thinking?'

THE HIEROPHANT

ARCANUM FIVE

Ask big questions

The Hierophant holds a double invitation. The first is to examine your influences. What experiences have shaped your beliefs and values? Whose rules are you following and what do you find yourself joining in with? Is this deepening your connection to the world and others or closing your mind? The second invitation is to cut out the middleman. Maybe you could explore and open directly to something bigger than you. What does it mean to accept that you're not the highest power in the universe? What if you tried seeking out this "something bigger". What might it teach you?

KEYWORDS

influences, beliefs, teachings, tradition, religion, idology, conformity, divinity, faith, spirituality

Reversed Card Question:
'What effect do my beliefs have on the way I treat other people?'

THE LOVERS

ARCANUM SIX

Explore loving behaviours

To love someone well is a choice we
must keep making. We make choices
day to day based on old dynamics
and beliefs that can stretch right
back to our childhood. This is how
we perpetuate patterns in our lives.
Use this card as a prompt to look at
your relationships. Are you reacting
in the same way over and over,
wondering why nothing changes? Or
is your pattern to sabotage, cheat,
fantasize or run away as a way to
avoid dealing with real life? As well
as choosing love and care over
dysfunction, you can also choose to
change the pattern.

KEYWORDS

relationships, love, emotion, choice,
connection, commitment, attraction,
chemistry, communication

Reversed Card Question:
*'Am I truly being loving here, or just
trying to get my own way?'*

THE CHARIOT

ARCANUM SEVEN

Accept your personal power

Let's talk about willpower. The Serenity Prayer says, "grant me the serenity to accept the things I cannot change, courage to change the things I can, and wisdom to know the difference". This is The Chariot. As life races us along, willpower can be an incredible tool to help us "course correct" and move us closer to what we want. It can also be a tremendous source of frustration and wasted energy. We can't control everything. When would it be wise to exert some willpower today and when do you need to let go?

KEYWORDS

willpower, control, force, movement, change, triumph, grit, wisdom, strength, mastery

Reversed Card Question:
'What same obstacles do I keep hitting?'

STRENGTH

ARCANUM EIGHT

Help yourself to feel safe

We all have impulses and behaviours that cause problems. True strength isn't about force – it's a softer, wiser kind of self-management. It's the strength to do what's right, to take care of yourself knowing that your wellbeing has an impact on others, and to see when you're doing things that aren't in your best interest. Giving yourself a hard time isn't going to help; change only comes when we feel safe. Your job is to make sure you're talking to yourself with love and support so that you feel safe enough to make different, better choices.

KEYWORDS

nonviolence, self-compassion, healing, patience, gentleness, sensitivity, acceptance, responsibility, safety, love

Reversed Card Question:
'How am I sending myself the message that I'm still not good enough?'

THE HERMIT

ARCANUM NINE

Make the most of solitude

Being alone can feel like a punishment, rejection. Or maybe you're someone who pulls solitude around you like a wall, to keep everyone and everything out. The Hermit suggests a wiser way to frame being alone – retreat not as avoidance or punishment but as something deep and fruitful. Turn toward solitude today as a way to let the jumble of your life and mind settle into stillness, like a clear pool. Lean on the things that give you strength to hold you steady as you watch, feel, learn. There is a breakthrough to be found here.

KEYWORDS

introspection, solitude, inner-wisdom, study, insight, retreat, focus, truth, meditation

Reversed Card Question:
'What am I trying to avoid feeling?'

THE WHEEL OF FORTUNE

ARCANUM TEN

Keep going

We love life when it's going well and hate when it isn't. The Wheel of Fortune reminds us that it's all one big endless cycle, as natural as the turning of the seasons. Change is going to happen whether you fight it or not, so why not use your energy for other things? While your life ebbs and flows, you have the option to just quietly get on with what matters to you, on good days and bad. Trust that the wheel will turn again and again, and you'll be OK. In the meantime, choose to be your own steady, consistent power and keep working with what you've got.

WHEEL OF FORTUNE

KEYWORDS

seasons, change, time, luck, resilience, faith, positivity, flexibility, impermanence

Reversed Card Question:
'What step could I take today to change my fate?'

JUSTICE

ARCANUM ELEVEN

Steer toward the good

Justice is a loaded, heavy word. How about balance? There are patterns and energies that run through life that are hard to notice. We do this, and that happens, someone else does that and this happens. How is this kind of cause and effect showing up in your life right now? Like it or not, we are all beings of action: everything we do and say triggers new chains of consequence and reaction. Whatever is happening, you can always decide to do something different, to set a new pattern in motion. We all have the power to make the world better, or worse.

KEYWORDS

choices, karma, power, responsibility, fairness, morality, balance, consequences, values

Reversed Card Question:
'What practical thing could I do instead of blaming or complaining?'

THE HANGED MAN

ARCANUM TWELVE

Wait and see

Sometimes the best thing is to simply wait. Feeling trapped is painful but things often just need more time. Accepting what is happening will feel uncomfortable. Your instinct will be to tense up, react, struggle, to try and fix things to make any bad feelings go away. In meditation, we call this "holding your seat" – it's about staying put, riding waves of thought, feeling and sensation. Today, just notice how you feel, your thoughts coming and going, any tension in your body. Breathe through it. Just wait. Trust that things are changing even if you can't see it.

KEYWORDS

stillness, endurance, acceptance, patience, surrender, rest, restriction, calm, discomfort, stasis

Reversed Card Question:
'Is change actually possible here? What's patience and what's denial?'

DEATH

ARCANUM THIRTEEN

Become something new

We all know death to be an ending, but Tarot teaches us a deeper truth. Death tells us that we must all change form many times. Our existence is always in motion and we don't get to hold anything still or unchanging for long. What is changing for you right now? You might feel grief, liberation, horror, relief, shock, panic. All feelings are valid. There is no easy answer here. No quick fix. Just honour what you must let go of, and, when you're ready, try to open, gently, to what your new form might be next. Think of caterpillars and butterflies.

KEYWORDS

change, renewal, loss, endings, beginnings, resistance, freedom, release, transformation

Reversed Card Question:
'What idea or memory do I keep clinging to?'

TEMPERANCE

ARCANUM FOURTEEN

Choose the middle way

Forever thinking in extremes – good/bad, all/nothing, this/not that – is how we keep ourselves stuck. It can lead us to make judgemental choices, make us feel powerless or drive deep wedges of division between us. He should...I can't...She never...Where are harsh words like this showing up in your life? Think of this card as a kind of softening, the middle way between extremes. What if everything wasn't as absolute as you think? Maybe it's time to experiment with a new way of doing things: one that holds a bigger, saner picture of possibility.

KEYWORDS

balance, fairness, non-judgement, compassion, humility, moderation, patience, healing, peace-making, compromise

Reversed Card Question:
'What am I convinced I'm right about? What if I'm not?'

THE DEVIL

ARCANUM FIFTEEN

Notice what controls you

We all have things we cling to even if they hurt us. Habits, beliefs, addictions, obsessions. It's a hard truth: the things that feel most comforting aren't necessarily helping you. It takes strength to look at your thoughts, patterns and coping strategies and to see that they're keeping you trapped, but there's a big, fresh world out there and it's calling you home. Are you thinking, reacting and behaving as the person you most aspire to be? The rest of your life is still one big possibility. Own up. Ask for help so you can learn how to make changes. Start today.

KEYWORDS

addiction, delusion, self-deception, self-sabotage, passivity, self-destruction, victimhood, dependence, liberation

Reversed Card Question:
*'What excuses do
I keep making?'*

THE TOWER

ARCANUM SIXTEEN

Trust in change

Change is frightening. We know it can come out of nowhere, pulling out the ground from beneath us, but this card isn't a portent of doom – it's simply a nudge to notice how anxious you feel about things that are uncertain. A lot of anxiety comes from us feeling sure there is only one right story and that anything else happening would be a disaster. What if that's not true? What if the tower is asking you to trust? Maybe life won't go as you've planned but you'll still be OK. Can you try on that thought today?

KEYWORDS

upheaval, uncertainty, trust, possibility, revelation, catastrophizing, assumptions, hope, breakthrough

Reversed Card Question:
'What story do I keep telling myself about the future?'

THE STAR

ARCANUM SEVENTEEN

Seek out inspiration

Having wishes and goals means having hope, but hope doesn't grow out of dry ground. When we feel hopeless, empty or uninspired, we need to seek out things that might help restore our sense that good things are possible. The Star represents everything that can rekindle a fresh sense of optimism, inspiration and creative drive. What do you need to start dreaming again? A change of scene? To try something new? Seek out things to nourish and stimulate you.

KEYWORDS

inspiration, hope, renewal,
creativity, dreams, energy,
meaning, purpose, motivation

Reversed Card Question:
*'What do I keep saying no to?
What if I said yes?'*

THE MOON

Embrace not knowing everything

Nothing in life can be fully understood and rationalized, however much we try to control it. There are mysteries and hidden sides to all things, ourselves included. It is this deep, pulling well of unsettling feelings, thoughts, energy that can make us feel off-kilter, wild, even afraid. Instead of seeing the unknowable as an enemy to be feared, fought or repressed, could you see it as an ally? What if you relaxed and opened to things being a mystery? Let go of your need to jump to conclusions, define or explain everything and just see what happens, what shifts and changes.

KEYWORDS

fears, mysteries, instinct, thoughts, anxiety, confusion, repression, projection, dreams

Reversed Card Question:
*'What am I afraid is true?
What am I afraid is not true?'*

THE SUN

ARCANUM NINETEEN

Practise joy

Feeling joy takes practice. If we're not careful, cynical or negative thought patterns, anxiety or constantly craving more can leave us unable to enjoy what's right in front of us. For joy to find us, we need to find ways to accept and welcome things as they are. This starts with seeing ourselves and our muddles with good humour – it's all OK. Next, look up. What's here? However we're feeling, we can always choose to embrace pleasure, beauty, playfulness. The best thing is, if you let the sun's energy *in*, it will start to shine *out* of you, too. Joyful people are a gift to the world.

KEYWORDS

joyfulness, action, vitality, energy, gratitude, play, optimism, positivity, celebration

Reversed Card Question:
'What things feed and reinforce a sense of misery in my life?'

JUDGEMENT

ARCANUM TWENTY

Try on a new attitude

The surprise in this card is that it's about resurrection. A new start. And right now, the only person who is judging you and holding you back from a new life is you! Self-criticism can be the biggest barrier to our growth, keeping us small. When we repeat the message that we're not good enough, we end up turning away from opportunities that could change our life. The Judgement card asks you to look honestly at yourself. Are all these "facts" about yourself true, or just old stories? If they're just old stories, maybe it's time to start writing a new one?

KEYWORDS

self-honesty, change, rebirth, growth, healing, transformation, self-help, introspection, action

Reversed Card Question:
'What am I most defensive about? What fear hides beneath it?'

THE WORLD

ARCANUM TWENTY-ONE

Celebrate the bigger picture

Other Tarot cards help us pull out a single thread to look at, but The World card is the cloth: all truths, all existence, everything, all at once. Today, try to catch a glimpse of this big, glorious picture. See where you are, how far you've come and all you have yet to learn. Embrace all of it. You are the story of the universe itself. Let your mind and heart be as expansive as it is. "There is even more to this than I can see." Say it with relief. Say it with exhilaration. Life is *big* and that is wonderful.

KEYWORDS

wholeness, perspective, expansion, complexity, completion, celebration, wisdom, non-duality, peace

Reversed Card Question:
'What are all the things that feel true to me right now even if they seem to contradict each other?'

THE MINOR ARCANA

QUEEN OF SWORDS

KING OF CUPS

The cards of the Minor Arcana show us the stuff of everyday: the stresses, activities, celebrations and concerns that ebb and flow throughout our ordinary lives. The cards are more structured than the Major Arcana, divided into suits – cups, wands, swords and pentacles – with each suit representing a different practical aspect of what it means to be a human living in the world.

Cups represent our feelings and emotions, what they can tell us, how they can inspire us and how they influence our thoughts and behaviour.

Wands are about our energy, the drive that keeps us moving to fulfil our dreams and our soul's calling.

Swords represent the power of minds, our thoughts, our ideas and our beliefs. They hold the power to both empower and to hurt.

Pentacles represent our behaviour: what we actually do. They reflect our habits, our work, our choices and, through that, our identity.

The number of the card also holds some significance:

Aces kick start new beginnings.

Twos are about our choices and partnerships.

Threes offer the safety of a grounding foundation.

Fours show structures that can trap us or free us.

Fives reflect our challenges and conflicts.

Sixes are about growth through love.

Sevens show us resilience, living in the real world.

Eights encourage us to reflect and commit.

Nines represent what we want and don't want.

Tens show us climaxes and revelations that help us start again.

Lastly, each suit contains four court cards, each of which embodies some of the main characteristics of their suit:

Pages are earnest beginners, still learning.

Knights want to move and make things happen.

Queens have learned inner confidence, wisdom and compassion.

Kings know how to turn deep wisdom into action.

Refer back to these added, hidden meanings often to enhance your understanding of the cards.

PAGE OF CUPS

KNIGHT OF WANDS

QUEEN OF SWORDS

KING OF PENTACLES

ACE OF CUPS

Refill your cup

We get to begin again however many times we choose. Today is a new chance for you to be your best self and to seek out good things to "fill your cup" with. How could you open more fully to what's around you? See what you can let flow in and flow out again. You can choose to be peaceful and light-hearted and to let things move you, delight you. There is holiness here and real healing. Imagine wide-open arms and laughing, easy joy.

Reversed Card Question:
"I tell myself I can only feel happy if... but is this true?'

opening
joy
flow
love
nourishment

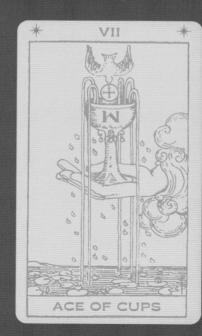

TWO OF CUPS

Ground love in truth

All relationships are an offering. We hope someone will say a warm "yes" to everything we are, and in turn, we can choose to say that same "yes" back. Relationships hit problems when we start to base our feelings on someone who isn't really there. We can distort people in our heads, only seeing what we wish for or turning them into a projection of our fears and insecurities. Today's challenge is to see the people in your life in their true fullness and to offer your real self in return. The best love is based in reality. That is the love you can trust.

Reversed Card Question:
'How could I better offer myself the love and care that I wish other people would give me?'

KEYWORDS

connection
vulnerability
partnership
honesty
commitment

THREE OF CUPS

KEYWORDS

friendship
celebration
affection
companionship
joy

Share joy

When life is stressful, we might find we only turn toward people in our lives to share woes. This card is an invitation to pull your loved ones close and to let a lightness break back into your conversations. Celebrate what's going well! Today, really notice the people you love and rekindle that flush of affection and closeness. What connects you and what do you enjoy doing together? Could you make some new time for that? This is how we bring out the best in ourselves and each other: by affirming what's good, joyful and appreciated.

Reversed Card Question:
'Who have I been pushing away lately?'

FOUR OF CUPS

Notice what's offered

We can get so lost in our feelings, wallowing, complaining or trying to make things go our way, that we miss what's right in front of us. In our tunnel vision, we forget to look up. The world around you is always offering you full cups, messages and opportunities that could change the story you're ruminating on. Are you paying attention? Could you open and take what's being offered? That might mean accepting help, taking responsibility or being willing to be wrong about something. What could you notice and respond to instead of sitting here passively, miserable?

Reversed Card Question:
'In what ways have I made suffering part of my identity? Is this who I want to be?'

KEYWORDS

discontent
apathy
rumination
negativity
excuse-making

FIVE OF CUPS

Hold on to what remains

Loss is one of the hardest feelings
to bear. When something is
truly gone or changed forever,
nothing can be done. All our usual
problem-solving tactics fail. We can
only free-fall in the gap loss leaves
and wait for the pain to ease. We
lose people we love; our bodies get
old or sick, our lives may change
before we're ready. And yet...*you*
are still here. See the two cups left
behind you? Not everything is lost.
You might not yet be ready to turn
toward what waits for you on the
other side of this, but for now just
know something more is here.

Reversed Card Question:
*'While I'm thinking about the past,
what is passing me by?'*

KEYWORDS

loss
disappointment
heartache
pessimism
regret

SIX OF CUPS

KEYWORDS

nostalgia
memories
forgiveness
compassion
positivity

Look back with love

We can be so hard on our younger selves, over-inflating our mistakes or wishing things had been different. This card asks you to take on the role of the sweetest, most loving person you can imagine and then to look back at your past with this mindset. Without resentment, judgement or regret, what goodness can you find? The past often contains forgotten treasures. Think of it as brave generosity. Be willing to set aside pain and disappointment for a while to reclaim and pass on precious gifts you may have left behind.

Reversed Card Question:

'What would my child-self think of the way I behave and live now?'

SEVEN OF CUPS

Root in reality

Thinking can be a real honey trap. In our heads, we can imagine anything we want, painting rosy pictures that only make us feel good, or proving ourselves right about how terrible something is by only focusing on what's wrong. It's all a mirage. In order to get what you need, you must come back to reality. Only real things can nourish you. Be courageous enough to find out what's actually true. Today, see that fantasies are just thoughts and air, and that negativity is often just as unrealistic. Living a life in your head isn't living at all.

Reversed Card Question:
'What one action could I take today that would reflect my deepest values?'

KEYWORDS

delusion
bias
self-deception
fantasizing
wishing

EIGHT OF CUPS

Move on with faith

Deciding to turn away from something that's hooked us takes real courage. We know, deep down, when a situation doesn't hold what we need, but when it promises something soothing or easy instead, it can be tempting to ignore our needs and just settle. If there's something missing in your life, you're not going to find it by keeping everything the same. To seek the missing cup means picking a direction and moving on with no guarantees you'll get a better deal. Hard, but the alternative is to stay stuck in an old life and an old self forever.

Reversed Card Question:
'What am I committed to?'

KEYWORDS

passivity
stagnation
avoidance
courage
faith

NINE OF CUPS

Explore what actually feels good

Are you chasing the right things? We all long to feel happy, but to feel genuine joy when good things happen, you need to have figured out what you actually want. If you don't know, you will always feel empty. Decide to investigate what truly makes you happy every day, the little things and the big. Dig deep. Maybe what actually makes you happy is a brilliant, unconventional surprise. Learn to get your heart, head *and* your behaviour authentically aligned and you have a chance to feel real contentment.

Reversed Card Question:
'What would 'enough' look like? Do I keep moving the finishing line?'

contentment

peace

happiness

fulfilment

appreciation

TEN OF CUPS

Enjoy where you are

We often imagine contentment as a "when" scenario: I will be happy *when* I don't feel this, *when* I have that thing, *when* this isn't happening anymore. This card challenges our assumptions about "happily ever after". What if a good life is simply finding the sweetness in the here and now? Peace can arrive when we accept ourselves and all our feelings – "this is happening" – and then look around at what we have now with a sense of true appreciation – "this is good." Today let go of the idea of "getting" anywhere at all. Root in the here and now.

Reversed Card Question:
'Who or what am I ignoring in my pursuit of a better life?'

KEYWORDS

gratitude
positivity
satisfaction
wholeness
acceptance

PAGE OF CUPS

Open to possibility

It's easy to become jaded, to reduce everything to endless bad news or to add a cynical "yeah, but". Maybe it's a defence mechanism to protect us from feeling too much, but when we cut off our willingness to be surprised, we also cut off our creativity and our capacity to be inspired and to change. Looking at it this way, isn't being a sensitive, big-feeling person a gift? Connect to the childlike optimist inside you today, the one who still believes in magic and is ready to learn something new. *Anything* can happen. What a hopeful thought.

Reversed Card Question:
'What am I making more complicated or dramatic than it needs to be?'

KEYWORDS

curiosity
creativity
openness
inspiration
sensitivity

PAGE OF CUPS

KNIGHT OF CUPS

Keep sight of what's good for you

Ah, romance. Maybe you're getting swept away by an actual person, or it could be an irresistible idea, or any compulsion that makes you feel like throwing caution to the wind. Wild abandon is sometimes exactly what we need to get out of a rut, but this card also suggests caution. Good things come from honest, committed action, not grand sentiments or transient feelings. This holds true for anything you're feeling enamoured by. Make your infatuation visible and grounded in reality and look for evidence that it's good for you. That's how we test whether risk is worth our while.

Reversed Card Question:
'With every gain comes loss. Have I explored all the pros and cons?'

KEYWORDS

infatuation
passion
fantasy
pleasure-seeking
risk

KNIGHT OF CUPS

QUEEN OF CUPS

Tune into your feelings

Our culture often derides people for being "too sensitive" but the Queen shows us that when we summon the strength to face our true feelings, we gain great power. Allowing ourselves to feel deeply grants us the ability to connect to and respond to the world around us. We can become a steady source of compassion, for ourselves and others. How might you seek to understand your shifting big feelings today? Writing them out is a good option. Focus on how *you* feel and what this feeling might be here to tell you. You don't need to take on other people's emotions as your own.

Reversed Card Question:
'Can I notice the difference between feeling and ruminating? One lets go; one holds on.'

KEYWORDS

emotion
compassion
care
strength
connection

QUEEN OF CUPS

KING OF CUPS

Express what's true

If we can learn to feel our emotions deeply without getting swept away by them, we can start to find powerful ways to utilize those feelings. Today, see that emotions are nothing to be afraid of but are part of your wisdom. Look for opportunities to tap your emotional depths to create art, poetry, writing, or to be a teacher or leader. By expressing your emotional truths with steadiness and honesty, you can help people change how they see themselves and their world. There is a real radiance to this way of living. We need more people like this.

Reversed Card Question:
'What if my flaws, insecurity and confusion were part of my gift to the world?'

KEYWORDS

creativity
self-expression
groundedness
influence
wisdom

✶ THE MAGICIAN ✶

ACE OF WANDS

Nurture this new spark

Something new is alight in you. The nudge of a new idea? A growing passion or conviction? A *"maybe I could"* goal or dream? Whatever it is, this card encourages you to take it seriously. It may still be just a tiny spark but, with time and attention, this new energy has the capacity to grow into something life-changing. Your first step might be making a plan, finding a teacher, doing some research, setting aside some time. Commit to nurturing it. This is the start of something important.

Reversed Card Question:
'What if I just took the first step right now and figured the rest out later?'

KEYWORDS

inspiration
ideas
potential
calling
spark

ACE OF WANDS

TWO OF WANDS

Choose something and commit

Do you have a choice to make? Are you hesitating, scared to commit to the wrong thing? Trying and failing isn't something to be afraid of. It's a far worse fate to live half-heartedly. If you're feeling disillusioned or let down by the reality of your life, see it as a chance to wake up. Have you been living a fantasy in your head rather than seeing things as they really are? What can you learn when you get real about what's happening? Could that tell you what to do next?

Reversed Card Question:
'Deep down, what do I really want?'

KEYWORDS

decisions
doubt
options
decisiveness
action

THREE OF WANDS

Embrace life's potential

There is a wistfulness here. Threes have a stability to them, so first let's notice that you are standing on solid ground. Your life is full of good things. So what is this feeling? A kind of hunger? There's nothing wrong with wanting more. To itch for adventure and to crave growth is part of being human, but we can get stuck hesitating, dreaming, sighing, with a kind of habitual, resigned hopelessness. You could spend your whole life lethargically waiting, wishing. If you need a message to just do the thing, then this is it.

Reversed Card Question:
'How am I keeping myself in my comfort zone?'

ambition
potential
adventure
change
movement

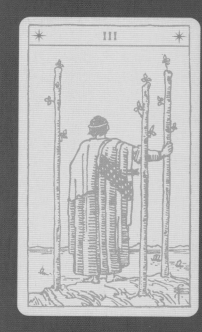

FOURS OF WANDS

Stop and celebrate

Celebration is a vital piece in the puzzle of how we learn how to feel happy. It reminds us of what's precious in our life, connects us with other people and lets us mark the passing of time. It's a way to touch base and slow down. What could you celebrate? There's no need to wait for something big to happen, but maybe something special *is* happening and you feel under pressure to minimize it or rush onto the next thing. Today is a day to pause and savour. Find a way to mark life's changes.

Reversed Card Question:
'What do I take for granted?'

KEYWORDS

celebration
appreciation
ritual
acknowledgement
joy

FIVE OF WANDS

Don't waste your energy

Are you wrestling with something you don't like? Whether you lash out or stew quietly, there's a big "don't want" mood about this card, a strong desire to get your own way to make things feel OK again. But is it getting you anywhere? Wands are all about energy. This card cautions you not to waste yours to a stalemate, resenting and fighting things you can't control. What if this was all a game you could take some pleasure in playing well, whatever is happening, rather than a struggle for dominance? There's a playfulness to be found here that's a lot less exhausting.

Reversed Card Question:
'What is this conflict teaching me about things that were once hidden?'

KEYWORDS

conflict
tension
struggle
drama
light-heartedness

SIX OF WANDS

Enjoy your success

What does winning mean to you? Maybe you demand victory at all times, becoming defensive or broken by the slightest hint of criticism. How dare anyone suggest you're wrong or spoil your good feelings! On the other hand, maybe you feel unable to show pride in your accomplishments and nothing is ever good enough. This card challenges you to take a lighter, more joyful attitude toward winning. Celebrate all your achievements with good humour. Success is just fun. It doesn't need to define everything and it doesn't determine your worth.

Reversed Card Question:
'Rather than trying to compete, what new definition of success could I come up with for myself?'

KEYWORDS

success
victory
self-assurance
confidence
celebration

SEVEN OF WANDS

Don't give up

Does it feel like you versus the world? There's anger in this card and that's nothing to be afraid of. Anger is energy. It can show you what's important to you and help you defend what's precious. Let this energy help you to declare that enough is enough and drive you to make a change or seek some help. Gather your resolve and pick yourself up. You don't need to lash out or blame yourself – destruction is not your only option. Decide to use your anger for good today.

KEYWORDS

courage
resolve
self-respect
challenges
resilience

Reversed Card Question:
'Am I clearly communicating what I need or am I just complaining?'

EIGHT OF WANDS

Follow the simplest path

We can spend our lives pushing against doors that won't open and miss the fact that there is opening waiting for us somewhere else. This is the card of movement. It says to look for the open door, the clear way, somewhere there is space. Then start moving... GO! Rather than picking the obstacle-filled path because you've stubbornly decided that it's the only option, today go with where you can make progress and build some momentum. Keep your wits about you and then you can change course as needed. Think of a motorbike speeding down that open road.

Reversed Card Question:
'Am I running towards something or away from something?'

KEYWORDS

action
momentum
kick-start
flow
focus

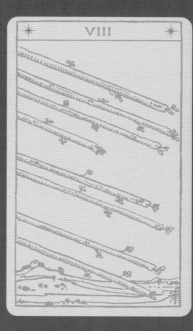

NINE OF WANDS

Stay true to yourself

When we have established good boundaries, we feel able to stay true to what is precious and meaningful to us. Boundaries are like your own personal code of conduct, something to help you live more authentically: "I will do this, I won't do that." These boundaries protect us from forces that try to turn us into something we don't want to be. We get lost when we try to use boundaries to control others or to try and ward off every uncomfortable feeling. Are you using your "yes" and "no" in the right way? What would be the bravest boundaries for you?

Reversed Card Question:
'Who or what could help me to keep going?'

KEYWORDS

strength
boundaries
conviction
self-protection
integrity

TEN OF WANDS

Lighten your load

The heaviest card. Our lives feel too much to bear some days but we put our heads down and trudge on. Let's stop and look at these sticks of yours. Have you taken on more than your share? Ten marks the end of a cycle so there is hope. You could put some of these sticks down or ask for help. Think about your boundaries today. Remember: setting boundaries is a kind of audit, a time to use your voice and power to say "yes" and "no" until you're only carrying the sticks you want. How much further could you get with a lighter load?

Reversed Card Question:
'Do I think my story is only valid if I'm struggling?'

PAGE OF WANDS

Just start and see what happens

When inspiration strikes, it feels like waking up. Suddenly, something new feels possible. Maybe *everything* feels possible. Don't let anyone try to squash this feeling in you. Seek out people who will encourage you. Just remember that you need to do something to get this ball rolling – don't keep it all in your head. It doesn't matter if you're not sure what you're doing yet or if things don't work out straight away. You're only just beginning and more inspiration will find you once you're moving. Take the smallest seed of possibility and run with it.

Reversed Card Question:
'Am I chasing a new goal to avoid persevering with an old one?'

KEYWORDS

vision
creativity
inspiration
passion
beginner

KNIGHT OF WANDS

Hold your nerve

To change things we have to uproot ourselves from solid ground and lean into what's unsteady and uncertain. The runaway-horse energy in this card reflects how that can feel both exhilarating and frightening. You're not entirely in control, but maybe that's what's needed to get you somewhere new? Today, don't be put off by that adrenaline surge as things shift around you. It doesn't mean anything has gone wrong. Things may be moving faster than is comfortable but what if that's part of the adventure? This might mean saying "yes" before you feel ready, taking a risk, following your gut.

Reversed Card Question:
'Rather than trying to do everything at once, what might one step at a time look like?'

KEYWORDS

impulsiveness
risk
excitement
change
uncertainty

KNIGHT OF WANDS

QUEEN OF WANDS

Protect and nurture positive energy

There is a kind of fire that feeds us, warms us and welcomes others; a slow, steady, productive sort of flame that we must keep tending to keep it burning. What fuels this kind of energy in you? It might be creativity, caring for others, nature – whatever it is, it has the power to draw people and good things closer to you. What threatens to put this fire out? The wrong voices in our life can, the wrong thoughts and habits, or being too busy. Think about how you could better protect and feed this good fire inside you with little twigs of time and attention.

Reversed Card Question:
'Whose opinion or mood controls me? How could I take back my power?'

KEYWORDS

willpower
strength
warmth
energy
self-awareness

QUEEN OF WANDS

KING OF WANDS

Use rebellion for good

Think heat, ignition, red and strong, the kind that makes things happen. This kind of intensity can change the world, for good and for ill. Its bold impulsivity stirs up the status quo and breaks all the rules. It can lead to the creation of powerful new things, or make you too hot to handle. It is the fire of poets, leaders, stars and innovators but, like all fire, it's not easy to control. It's time to see your energy and take responsibility. How could you better ignite and wield this force within you? What change could it fuel, what could it burn away and what could it reveal?

Reversed Card Question:
'How could I better support others rather than try to leave them behind?'

KEYWORDS

intensity
passion
rebellion
vision
charisma

KING OF WANDS

ACE OF SWORDS

Stop deliberating

This ace marks the opportunity to embrace a new, decisive way of thinking. Maybe you've been feeling confused or muddled, trying to hold too many ideas or truths at once, or you're resisting "picking a side". Some days do call for us to see the bigger picture, but if we never make our minds up, we can spend our whole life passively sitting on the fence, never taking action on anything. This card says: make a decision about what's right and true and act. You can always change your mind as you go.

Reversed Card Question:
'How is wishful thinking steering me off course?'

KEYWORDS

clarity
breakthrough
strength
action
motivation

ONE OF SWORDS

TWO OF SWORDS

Look at all the evidence

Making a good choice is about choosing the most helpful things to focus on. Our heads can feel like a maelstrom, pulling us this way and that. It can be easy to just close our eyes and shut down. When something overwhelms you but you know you must make a choice, try to take the blindfold off. Lay out all your evidence, thoughts and interpretations. Which story makes you feel strong and capable? Which thoughts keep you stuck, trapped and miserable? Reinforce the good thoughts and the right choice becomes much more obvious.

Reversed Card Question:
'Is gathering more and more information just keeping me stuck?'

KEYWORDS

decisions
stalemate
blocks
denial
evidence

THREE OF SWORDS

Be honest about how you feel

We can't think or avoid our way
out of pain. Sometimes life simply
pierces us. This is the pain of
heartbreak, of profound grief,
deep hurt. The relief in this card
is that it says: don't cover anything
up or power through. In order
to move through us and not get
stuck, feelings need to be felt and
expressed. You are allowed to be
vulnerable and to have needs. As
you let sensation flow through,
notice that your thoughts might be
complex. There are three swords,
not one. Maybe there is sadness
and also fear? How about anger?
Acknowledge all of it. This is how
to heal.

Reversed Card Question:
'Who could I choose to forgive?'

KEYWORDS

heartbreak
pain
wounds
release
acceptance

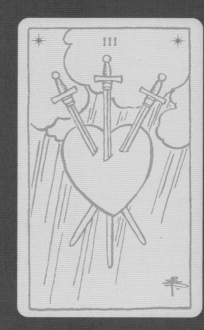

FOUR OF SWORDS

Rest your mind

A society obsessed with productivity and self-improvement puts us under a lot of pressure to be on the go all the time. This card is a firm hand on your shoulder telling you to stop. It's not just our bodies that need rest, it's our minds. When you're resting, are you really resting? Or are you just staying busy in a different way? True rest – actually putting everything down – can feel uncomfortable or scary, but it's in these still moments that we most often find sudden clarity and insight. Notice if your mind and body are a runaway train right now. It's safe and right to stop.

Reversed Card Question:
'Which of my current habits make me feel more stressed?'

KEYWORDS

rest
stillness
restoration
withdrawal
detox

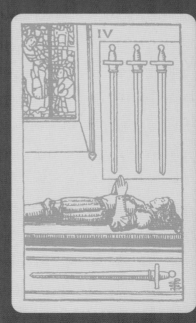

FIVE OF SWORDS

Take responsibility

There's a real sense of conflict in this card. Do you feel like the justified victor? Or do you feel like you've been treated unfairly? Either way, you're probably telling yourself a story about why you're the one who's right. This card can be a good encouragement to watch how your thoughts and words are escalating the situation. What are the plain facts? Whether you feel righteous or wretched, remember you have choices. You could talk this out with someone neutral. You could walk away. You could even make peace. You can decide to change the story.

Reversed Card Question:
'If I'm honest with myself, who am I hurting here?'

conflict
bitterness
blame
destruction
choice

SIX OF SWORDS

Don't wait to feel ready

We often wait to "feel ready" when we know that change is going to hurt or when we feel that we're not good enough as the person we are right now. This card invites you to pick up your baggage, your wounds and your fears, exactly as you are, and start anyway. It might feel frightening or hopeless to begin with, but by taking small, sensible steps toward what you need and want for your life, things around you will start to change. Who knows what's on the other side of this? Shall we go see? Make an action plan then get moving. You can do this.

Reversed Card Question:
'What have I decided is completely out of my control? Is it really?'

KEYWORDS

change
transition
recovery
future
hope

SEVEN OF SWORDS

Be honest with yourself

The card of betrayal. There is no getting away from the fact that other people do let us down in life: they lie, cheat and hurt. But it can be far easier to point fingers of blame than to admit that we don't always act well either. Today might be a good day to think about authenticity. Do your actions match your values and promises right now? Are you telling the whole truth or using half-truths to control the narrative or to cover something up? No matter what others do to us, however scared we may feel, we betray ourselves when we don't live with honesty and integrity.

Reversed Card Question:
'What secret weighs on me most heavily? What could I do if I wasn't carrying that burden?'

KEYWORDS

deception
betrayal
self-honesty
authenticity
manipulation

EIGHT OF SWORDS

Don't jump to conclusions

We can end up stuck when we believe in one "right" way to do things but can't seem to live up to that ideal, when we believe that taking action is going to make us feel something we don't like, and when we repeatedly tell ourselves stories about who we are and what things mean. Our thoughts can hem us in until we can't move. The key to this card is remembering that beliefs *are* thoughts, not reality. Take the blindfold off. Are you really trapped, or is there actually a lot of space here? A good question to ask is, "What if...?" Try on some new ideas.

Reversed Card Question:
'How might freeing myself from negativity help other people?'

KEYWORDS

restriction
helplessness
negativity
rumination
excuses

NINE OF SWORDS

Remember this isn't the end

A card of nightmares; the kind of mental anguish that feels like the end of everything. But what if this isn't the end of the story? It's time to find out. Do anything but sit there in the dark playing it over in your mind. Get up. Do something, anything; just something to get you moving. Look for fresh air. There is plenty of room here yet for things to play out in ways you can't predict. What might happen if you got out of bed, looked around you, expressed some of these thoughts out loud, got some help? Why don't you try and see what happens?

Reversed Card Question:
'If I talked to someone else the way I'm talking to myself right now, how would it affect them?'

KEYWORDS

despair
distress
panic
rumination
self-sabotage

TEN OF SWORDS

Turn toward healing

Ouch. Take a deep breath. Remember that swords represent your mind, so even though you may feel pierced through, you are safe in this moment. This intensity *will* pass. More hopeful still – Tens signify an ending. You might have been hurt or frightened, deeply, but it's done. So what next? Next you start the bloody, slow business of pulling out those swords, one at a time, and healing your wounds. That means taking each painful thought and looking at it, bravely. What needs to happen so you can start to heal? The best way to start is to speak to yourself with love and kindness. You deserve care.

Reversed Card Question:
'What old wound do I keep picking at?'

KEYWORDS

crisis
defeat
endings
pain
healing

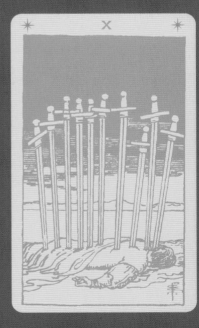

PAGE OF SWORDS

Check your blind spots

Passion can be wonderful, but now might be a good time to check in. Are you using your ideas and opinions to inspire others, or to try and control everything? When we feel pulled to righteous action or feel an urgent need to change things, sometimes we're just stuck in wound-up, fight-or-flight mode, reacting to an enemy that isn't really there. Endlessly defending our thoughts and opinions can lead us to have a very cloudy view of things. Can you release the tight hold you have on everything just a little to help you see things more clearly?

Reversed Card Question:
'Instead of trying to be the best at everything, what's one thing I could do well?'

KEYWORDS

enthusiasm
opinions
defensiveness
self-expression

PAGE OF SWORDS

KNIGHT OF SWORDS

Practise focus

Modern life actively discourages us from commitment. Instead, it encourages us to rush, multi-task, to instantly swap out anything that feels uncomfortable for something better and to constantly search for something new to entertain or soothe us. Single-pointed focus is a kind of superpower: it gives you an edge. What in your life would benefit from this kind of commitment of focus? It isn't an easy thing to achieve, so what could help you ward off distraction? Just deciding that you're going to stay really present with what you're doing right now is a start. Slowing down helps.

Reversed Card Question:
'What do I need to cut away to make the future I want more likely to happen?'

KEYWORDS

single-mindedness
commitment
determination
focus
action

KNIGHT OF SWORDS

QUEEN OF SWORDS

Examine what's really true

The truth is often more complex than we imagine. Your wisest, most experienced self knows how to see the bigger picture and to see where drama and exaggeration are muddying the view. When we feel insecure, we can get pulled back into that childish part of us that judges and clings to absolutes, but the Queen represents that older, self-assured, calm part of you that values wisdom over winning. If you can take responsibility, refuse to be a victim and instead cut away what's delusional, unhelpful or untrue, you can hold real power to change your life and do good.

Reversed Card Question:
'What assumptions am I making about the person I've been judging lately?'

clarity
independence
strength
wisdom
truth

QUEEN OF SWORDS

KING OF SWORDS

Notice what has your attention

Where's your head at? It's a matter of life or death because what you focus on moment to moment will decide what lives, what grows and what dies. The way to feed something is to give it attention. The way to kill something is to turn away from it. Both hold the potential to heal or to hurt, especially if you're running on autopilot. If you can learn to see what you're actually doing, with discernment and responsibility, you will get to step into your true power as an adult. It's also your best opportunity to shape the life you most want.

Reversed Card Question:
'What good things have I been cutting out of my life lately?'

focus
insight
responsibility
decision-making
honesty

KING OF SWORDS

ACE OF PENTACLES

Say "yes"

All great changes start with noticing that we're being offered something. Right now, the world might be offering you a new insight or vision, some time or spare cash, someone to help or just something really pleasurable to help you feel happy – it could be anything. If you're hoping to make a change or to start something new, keep your eyes open for what resources and possibilities are all around you today. You might be surprised at how abundant and generous the world actually is. Don't be afraid to take what's here. Say "yes". Say "thank you". Then use it to do something good.

Reversed Card Question:
'What do I keep running out of? How could I better manage my resources?'

KEYWORDS

opportunity
gifts
abundance
support
change

TWO OF PENTACLES

Don't take anything too seriously

When there's a lot to think about or do, we can feel wrung-out and overwhelmed, even self-pitying. We forget that being busy offers a wonderful opportunity to be playful and to enjoy being alive. What could you learn from the juggler? To bend and flex, balance, laugh and have fun. Nothing needs to be a big deal today. Yes, you'll need to focus and you might drop some balls, but that doesn't matter. You can always try again. Let go of perfectionism and just enjoy this lively dance between you and the universe.

Reversed Card Question:
'Am I stressing myself out with things that are actually optional?'

KEYWORDS

busyness
flexibility
priorities
energy
balance

THREE OF PENTACLES

Invite others to join you

When we try to do everything on our own, our path gets very dark and narrow. When we connect with others, we find light and space. Maybe there you'll learn something new, or maybe you'll act as a catalyst in someone else's journey. What happens if you stop seeing your dreams and ambitions as a solo affair? Maybe the way to success is to do things together. Think about who you could ask to join you today. What if you're not just here to do your important work, but to help others with theirs, too?

Reversed Card Question:
'What might change if I trusted that everyone around me was doing their best?'

KEYWORDS

collaboration
teamwork
community
synergy
contribution

FOUR OF PENTACLES

Trust in abundance

We often feel stuck when we believe that there isn't enough to go around: enough money, success, luck, love. We obsess over what we think we're lacking or might lose. Worse, we feel resentful of others if they get something first. Is there an area in your life that makes you clench up defensively when you think about it? What if there was simply more abundance in the world than you believe and the way to access it was to open and be more generous? It might feel scary and counter-intuitive but be brave: give away some of what feels scarce in your life and see what happens.

Reversed Card Question:
'Rather than desiring more, what could I decide is 'good enough' today?'

hoarding
obsession
resentment
fear
trust

FIVE OF PENTACLES

Let in the good

Feeling like you've lost everything can freeze you solid. You might feel totally alone, like the universe itself has kicked you out of all that is joyful. When something bad happens, you might tell yourself that you don't deserve good things, that you're being punished, that you're broken, unwelcome and irredeemable, so you stay where you are, stuck in the cold and the dark. But what if you didn't need to stay frozen and hungry? You haven't been banished: light, care, change are still here. You are always welcome to step back into life. There is plenty here still waiting for you.

Reversed Card Question:
'What if recovery is already happening and I just can't see it yet?'

KEYWORDS

loss
suffering
hardship
depression
self-punishment

SIX OF PENTACLES

Explore reciprocity

The idea of giving and receiving is often more complex than we acknowledge. We can give or receive with no expectations or strings attached, or it can come with a deeper agenda. Are you more the giver or the receiver right now? Today, think about what lies underneath that dynamic. Are you giving but resenting it? Receiving but feeling squashed? Hoarding, or exhausting yourself? Look out for power imbalances, hidden messages and battles for control. What might you need to do to create more balanced, reciprocal relationships? How could you give and receive in a healthier way?

Reversed Card Question:
'What do I really want to happen? How could I stop playing games?'

KEYWORDS

relationships
reciprocation
generosity
gratitude
power

SEVEN OF PENTACLES

Notice what's going well

This is an invitation to rest and reflect on how well things are going. Are things, actually, just fine? This is a good chance to challenge your attitude of "never enough" and take some time for gratitude. Even if you do need to alter course, it's no big deal. Just look at your patterns and habits with compassion for clues about what to work on next. And remember: you're allowed to feel good! You don't have to wait for a big win or always obsess over the next thing. If resting or celebrating the small stuff are hard, what are you telling yourself that means you can never stop or feel satisfied? Are those stories true?

Reversed Card Question:
'What am I pouring energy into that isn't improving or changing? What could I do differently?'

KEYWORDS

reward
satisfaction
contentment
gratitude
assessment

EIGHT OF PENTACLES

Commit to showing up

How often do you manage to settle down and do real work on things that matter to you? If you're attempting any kind of regular practice, you'll know how hard it is. It's important to work out what's getting in the way. Often it's perfectionism and a fear of failing. We set the bar so high that we freeze up under the pressure. But progress only comes if you actually show up and do the work. Mistakes are OK. Can you practise having disappointing days and still showing up again the next day? Trust the process. If you can just keep coming back and trying again, something good will happen.

Reversed Card Question:
'Are my rules and standards realistic for the life I have right now?'

KEYWORDS

commitment
repetition
practise
discipline
trust

NINE OF PENTACLES

Invest in your future

Gardens remind us that for good growth, we must water, prune, weed, try again. When the harvest comes, gardens help us pause and appreciate our reward. No accomplishment ever happens by accident. That leaves room for both hope *and* pride. So is your life right now feeling barren? Think seeds, patience and commitment. If you see that things around you are actually quite comfortable and full, what could you pick and enjoy? Watch out for boredom and impatience that will make you want to dig everything over too soon. The best gardens aren't rushed.

Reversed Card Question:
'What do I resent life not giving me? Does my happiness really depend on it?'

KEYWORADS

abundance
reward
pleasure
independence
accomplishment

TEN OF PENTACLES

Celebrate your interconnection

Today, remember that you belong. You belong to yourself, to your body, to people around you, to your neighbourhood, to the wider world, the trees, the birds, the flowers. You are already in a relationship with *all* these things. Isn't that wonderful? When we feel cut off or excluded, it's often because we've forgotten that we are fundamentally joined up with everything and everyone around us. This is a day to see and celebrate your interconnectedness. What overlooked relationship could you deepen and grow?

Reversed Card Question:
'Who do I hurt when I refuse to feel satisfied?'

KEYWORDS

connection
community
relationships
abundance
appreciation

PAGE OF PENTACLES

Make time for learning

Studying something is a kind of devotion: a way for us to honour that life is rich and interesting and that we don't know everything. When you decide to learn, you have a chance to open your heart as well as your mind, to expand your understanding of the world and yourself and discover what feels most meaningful to you. Learning helps us because it encourages us to actually do things. You will have to try stuff out, practise, listen, respond. How could you embrace the deeper attitude of a student today? What could it inspire you to *do*?

Reversed Card Question:
'Have I made learning feel like a chore? How could I bring back the fun?'

KEYWORDS

learning
openness
practise
study
apprenticeship

PAGE OF PENTACLES

KNIGHT OF PENTACLES

Hold your course

Because it's normal for our minds to race and our emotions to fluctuate, it can be hard to stay steady. It can even be tempting to let ourselves get carried away by this or that because we know consistency and hard work are boring. In order to get anywhere, sometimes we need to turn away from drama and just get on with it. This card is a challenge to simply knuckle down and work hard until the work is done. The energy here is slow but determined. No excuses, just plod plod plod. Yes, it's dull, but the results will be worth it.

Reversed Card Question:

'Am I doing things a certain way because it actually helps, or just out of habit or duty?'

KEYWORDS

consistency
focus
routine
dedication
effort

KNIGHT OF PENTACLES

QUEEN OF PENTACLES

Give with confidence

Once we understand that there's more than enough goodness to go around and that we can create our happiness no matter what, we gain the freedom and strength to become truly generous rather than self-protective. All of us want to be kinder and more caring. Today, turn toward the world and people around you and practise what you know to be right. Give your time, patience, your good humour, your problem-solving skills and share whatever resources you can. Living out your values is the path to real self-esteem.

Reversed Card Question:
'Who else suffers if I don't tend to my own needs?'

KEYWORDS

self-sufficiency
resourcefulness
confidence
generosity
compassion

QUEEN OF PENTACLES

KING OF PENTACLES

Focus on practical next steps

The idea of taking responsibility
can feel heavy, but what if
you thought of it as a kind of
power? Life is fundamentally
unpredictable. You can't control
what each day brings, but you
can choose what you're going
to do next. By focusing on your
own actions, your life becomes
something you can craft, moment
to moment, rather than something
that just happens to you. You get
to say, "Whatever happens, I've
got my own back." How might life
change if you refused to wallow
or make excuses and instead kept
coming back and asking, "OK, now
what can I do?"

Reversed Card Question:
*'Has my self-sufficiency tipped into
selfishness? How could I redress
the balance?'*

KING OF PENTACLES

CARD SPREADS AND STORIES

QUEEN OF SWORDS

III

THE EMPRESS

ACE OF WANDS

Once the cards start to feel like familiar friends, you might like to introduce spreads into your practice. A Tarot spread is just a way of laying out multiple cards in a particular pattern or structure in order to weave multiple card meanings together. There are a number of traditional spreads that you'll see used in Tarot examples, such as the Celtic Cross, but there are no official ways of laying out the cards and no particular spread is needed to make the cards "work" better. Being inventive with Tarot spreads, rather than sticking to them like a prescription, is one of the best ways to introduce creativity into your practice and make it your own. Think of spreads as story-crafting.

WHAT TO DO

Start by choosing one area of your life or a specific situation you'd like to explore. Perhaps it's something you're worried about, or a relationship or some aspect of your work or career – just whatever you'd like more clarity on. Then, in the same way that you'd pick your daily card (see page 18), pick out the number of cards that you'd like to work with and lay them out in front of you.

TWO-CARD SPREADS

The simplest and most natural evolution from a one-card draw is two cards! Introducing the extra dynamic of a second card is the perfect way to broaden your understanding of a situation and add additional context and clues. What two different aspects of your experience, thoughts, behaviour or difficulty could you explore?

Maybe your two-card story could look something like this. Just choose one set or pair from the list to start with, then with your eyes closed, pick out one card from your deck for each aspect. What other pairs can you think of?

The first card you draw	The second card you draw
The surface situation	The deeper truth
Now	Next
Me	Another person
Where I am	What I'm missing
One choice available to me	A second choice
My strengths	My blind spots
What I know	What I need to learn
What I think is happening	What is actually happening

THREE-CARD SPREADS

Here we have the chance to add an additional "plot point". Can you see how each additional card adds a new layer of story?

Again, decide in advance which story "triplet" you'd like to explore or write your own, close your eyes and pick your cards.

First card	Second card	Third card
Where I've come from	Where I am	Where I'm headed
What's happening	What's getting in the way	Where I need to be
What I'm doing well	What isn't working	How I need to change
What I'm thinking about	What I'm doing	The consequence
What I want	What I need	What I need to be careful of
Influences from the past	Influences in the present	The teacher I need next
Who I was	Who I am now	Who I could be
Me	Another person	What unites us

SPREAD SHAPES
AND PATTERNS

Three-card spreads are a good opportunity to start bringing in a sense of shape and design to your story spread. Think about the examples above and consider how you could place your three cards on the table in front of you.

- Do they follow an order through time like a line?

- Perhaps you'd like to lay them out like a triangle that leads the story round in a circle.

- You might like to lay out two cards with one that acts as the obstacle or wall between them.

- Maybe your three cards could be like a staircase climbing toward something higher.

- Does one card "dominate" the others, rising over them?

- Or is there a hidden influence that lies below the others?

There are no wrong answers. What makes sense to you? What would best illustrate the story you are exploring?

You might like to design your spread in advance, drawing your design on a piece of paper to lay your cards over as you pull them from the deck. Or you could lay out the cards first and see what shape they seem to lend themselves to as you explore their meanings. Keep track of your designs and story questions in your notebook so that you can use them again or refine them in the future.

As you get more confident, you can experiment with four, five and six card spreads...or even more! Four-card spreads lend themselves nicely to a balanced square, five to a star or flower shape, and six cards to a hierarchical pyramid in a 3-2-1 arrangement. With your situation in mind, you could even think of laying out multiple cards like the panels of a graphic novel and "reading" them like a comic book. You could lay out one card for each day of the week in advance and see how/if that story plays out, or the same for the months of a new year. The possibilities really are endless so have fun with it.

AN EXAMPLE READING

Let's say that I had a conversation with a friend yesterday that has left me feeling insecure. I'm not sure why - she didn't say anything hurtful - but something about the interaction is playing on my mind and I feel raw and small. What three aspects of the situation might help me gain some insight into how I'm feeling?

We could try:

- My reality

- My friend's reality

- The thought that's getting in the way of me seeing clearly

I'll draw three cards, focusing on each of these aspects in turn, placing the 'thought' card between me and my friend to symbolise the obstruction. Have a look at the reading on the opposite page – what story do the cards tell?

My reality	The thought that's getting in the way of me seeing clearly	My friend's reality

The Emperor	*Seven of Cups*	*King of Wands*
I'm having to be very strong in my life and shoulder a great deal of responsibility.	I wish things could be different for me. It's not fair - it's all so easy for her. If only I was more like her, my life would be better.	My friend is full of energy, charisma and drive. People are drawn to her and she's receiving a lot of praise and attention.

WHAT TO ASK NEXT

Yes, that feels true. Now, I'll redraw and replace the middle card, asking:

What perspective could help me feel better?

Take a look at the revised spread opposite and how this card changes the reading.

I love the three strong figures that complete our spread! Wishful thinking, resentment and comparison were warping my perspective. I see now that I am my own kind of leader: one who's quietly creating a better life for myself day by day. I can feel proud of my strength and courage.

My reality	What perspective could help me feel better?	My friend's reality

The Emperor	*King of Pentacles*	*King of Wands*
I'm having to be very strong in my life and shoulder a great deal of responsibility.	Maybe my actions aren't so visible to others, but I hold a different kind of power. I can keep making good choices and steer my life in a positive direction.	My friend is full of energy, charisma and drive. People are drawn to her and she's receiving a lot of praise and attention.

GOING
DEEPER

ACE OF PENTACLES

VII

THE CHARIOT

KNIGHT OF WANDS

READING FOR
OTHER PEOPLE

If Tarot really gets under your skin and starts to become a part of your life, it is natural to begin thinking about doing readings for other people. If your friends and family know that you use Tarot cards, they might even ask you directly if you will read for them.

If this is something you'd like to consider, please do take the following thoughts to heart.

Tarot touches on some of our deepest human wounds, dysfunctions and psychology. Just as counsellors and psychologists must train to help people face their darkness and joys with skill, Tarot readers also have a responsibility to handle others with training and care. Remember that your interpretations of the cards could have a big impact on someone's mood, sense of safety, hope and behaviour. Tread carefully. Perhaps Tarot could be a wonderful accompaniment to an additional therapeutic practice you may like to train in.

All people have the ability to read Tarot for themselves and draw their own insights. Rather than telling people what their cards mean, how could you help others build their own relationship with the cards? Perhaps a reading is something you could do together, sharing ideas and lending your understanding, rather than a message you deliver.

> **You have something unique and valuable to add to Tarot's potential.**

Before reading for others, I would encourage you to study Tarot in depth and to take your time. Read widely, both classic Tarot texts and new. Tarot is a rich tradition and it's evolving all the time. Rather than simply memorizing and repeating other people's interpretations or approaches, how could you bring your own wisdom to a reading? You have something unique and valuable to add to Tarot's potential. If you do decide to read for others, don't be afraid to try new things or shake up tradition, but root down in what's come before you.

TAROT AS A WAY OF LIFE

My hope is that Tarot can be a companion to you. A consistent anchor and sanctuary that can bring a real sense of support to your life. But your daily Tarot reading is just the beginning. Here are some more ways you can weave the cards into your way of living and seeing:

TAROT SHRINES AND TALISMANS

If one particular card seems to resonate with you more deeply, especially if you find it keeps coming up in your readings, why not find ways to bring it into the wider world with you? You could set aside a place on a shelf dedicated to your card and begin to collect

and gather things to represent it, or pick one small thing to carry around with you. What objects come to mind? Any colours? What key words? What about animals or plants? Draw things, find, make.

ELEMENTS

Many of the cards, particularly in the Minor Arcana, have an element associated with them. Cups speak to water, wands to fire, swords to air and pentacles to Earth. Each day that you draw a card, look for the element within it and then make time to connect to that element in your surroundings that day, using all of your senses.

ART AND WRITING

Tarot cards can be a wonderful catalyst for creative work. Perhaps you'd like to try and draw or paint your own version of your daily card, in an abstract or figurative style. You could write about the characters and the situation you see within a card, like looking through a window into another world. See each card as a deep pool. How could you dive in with your imagination? What could you draw back out to show the world?

A TAROT BLESSING

When I first began exploring the Tarot, I did so secretly, feeling very unsure and nervous. Tarot felt like something 'other' and I often felt like I was trespassing in a world I didn't really belong to. My greatest hope with this book is that you can start your Tarot adventure knowing that you belong here already, that the cards are old friends waiting to welcome you, and that you can bring your whole self and life to the cards and find nothing but love and gentle wisdom returned to you.

May you be brave
May you steer towards your truth
May you always be kind to yourself
May you find joy and hope in every day